**Tobias Picker**
b.1954

# Car Aria
from *An American Tragedy*
for Baritone and Piano

## Libretto by Gene Scheer
Based on a story by Theodore Dreiser

ED 30044

www.schott-music.com

Mainz · London · Madrid · New York · Paris · Prague · Tokyo · Toronto
© 2010 SCHOTT HELICON MUSIC CORPORATION, New York · Printed in USA

# TOBIAS PICKER

## Car Aria

from *An American Tragedy*
for Baritone and Piano

Schott Helicon Music Corporation

ED 30044

# Car Aria

from "An American Tragedy"

(version for Baritone)

Gene Scheer

Tobias Picker

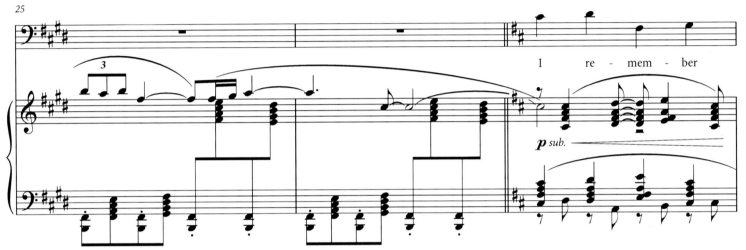

I re-mem-ber

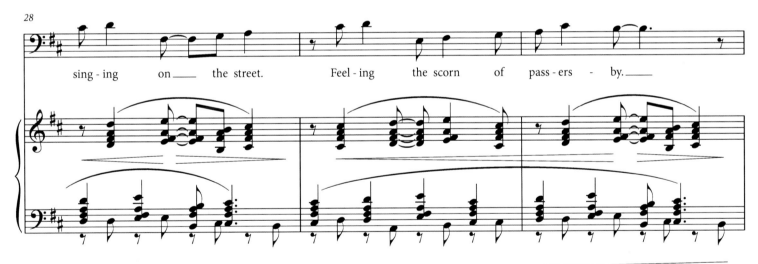

sing-ing on____ the street. Feel-ing the scorn of pass-ers - by.____

Feel - ing I'd nev - er get out, nev - er____ get to try.

Hymns and prayers, hymns and prayers. Noth-ing___ but dis - dain-ful stares.___

But look at me now! Fif - teen a

week and run-ning___ this floor!___ Hard work___ and hope.___ A few years___ from now___

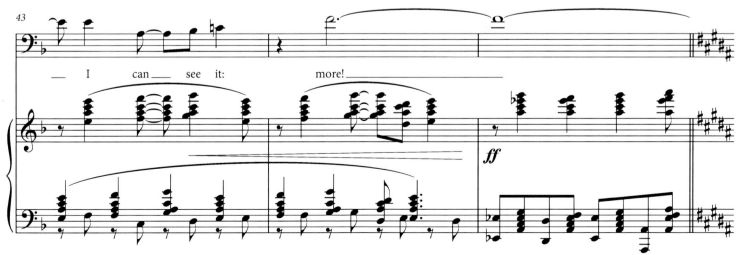

___ I can___ see it: more!___

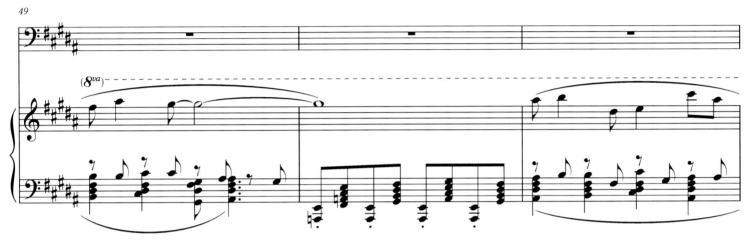

That pret-ty girl.___ What was her name? I be-lieve, I be-lieve, yes, Ro-ber-ta that's

but ease___ as I climb each hill.___ Grav-i-ty___ can't...

Grav - - i - ty___ can't hold___ me still.___

To own a mo-tor-car!___ That mo-tor-car!___

Bur - gun - dy red___ with wood-en trim!___

**Schott Helicon Music Corporation**

**254 West 31st Street, 15th Floor**
**New York, NY 10001**
**Tel: 212 461 6940**
**Fax: 212 810 4565**
**ny@schott-music.com**

HL 49018269
ISBN: 978-1-61780-330-7

ISBN-13: 978-1-61780-330-7
Distributed By
HAL LEONARD
49018269    9 781617 803307